FROM SCREEN TO SHELF

From Screen to Shelf

THE ESSENTIAL GUIDE TO PROP COLLECTING FOR BEGINNERS

Asaf Iqbal

PRESTIGE QUILL

Prestige Quill Publishing

Contents

1

Introduction to Prop Collecting

From Screen to Shelf: the Essential Guide to Prop Collecting for Beginners

Introduction to Prop Collecting

Understanding Props

Props are an essential component of any movie, TV show, or stage production. They may not always steal the spotlight like the actors or the breathtaking set design, but props play a crucial role in bringing a story to life. They are the unsung heroes that add depth, authenticity, and visual interest to a scene. From a simple coffee cup in a sitcom to an intricate sword in a fantasy epic, props have the power to transport viewers into the world of the story and make it feel tangible.

So, what exactly are props? In the simplest terms, props are objects that actors interact with on screen or on stage. They can be anything from furniture, clothing, and vehicles to weapons, jewellery, or even a tiny trinket that holds sentimental value. Props serve multiple purposes. Firstly, they provide visual cues to the audience, helping to establish the time period, location, or character traits.

For example, a vintage typewriter on a desk instantly transports us to the past, while a sparkling diamond ring suggests wealth and status.

Props can also be used to enhance a character's personality or tell a story within a story. Imagine a detective lighting a cigarette with a zippo lighter engraved with a mysterious symbol – it immediately sparks curiosity and hints at a hidden backstory.

The importance of props in storytelling cannot be overstated. They serve as tools for the actors, helping them to physically embody their characters and make their performances more convincing. Props can also convey emotions and convey a character's state of mind. A broken mirror, shattered by a character in a fit of rage, symbolises their inner turmoil and reflects their fragmented psyche. In this way, props become visual metaphors, enriching the narrative and providing deeper layers of meaning.

Now, you might be wondering how props come to be. Well, the creation of props is a collaborative effort between prop masters, set designers, and artisans. These talented individuals work behind the scenes to design, build, and source the perfect props for a production. They carefully consider the needs of the script, the director's vision, and the overall aesthetic of the project. Sometimes, props are sourced from existing objects, while other times, they are custom-made from scratch. Regardless of their origin, props require meticulous attention to detail and a keen eye for authenticity.

After all, a historically accurate prop can transport audiences back in time, while a poorly executed prop can be jarring and break the illusion.

In the world of prop collecting, enthusiasts go beyond the realm of passive viewership and become active participants in the magic of storytelling. Collecting props allows fans to connect with their favourite movies, TV shows, and stage productions on a deeper level. It is a way to bring a piece of that world into their own lives and create a personal connection with the stories, characters, and the creative process. Whether it's owning a replica of Harry Potter's wand or a piece of the Iron Throne from Game of Thrones, collecting props is a way to express one's passion and celebrate the artistry behind the scenes.

But where does one begin their prop collecting journey? How does one acquire these coveted treasures? Fear not, for this book will guide you through the exciting and sometimes daunting world of prop collecting. We will explore the ins and outs of acquiring, preserving, and appreciating props. From setting goals and determining budgets to evaluating sellers and ensuring authenticity, we will equip you with the knowledge and confidence to start building your own prop collection.

Throughout this book, we will share practical tips, personal anecdotes, and stories from experienced collectors. We want to make this journey engaging and relatable, because after all, prop collecting is as much about the thrill of the hunt as it is about the final acquisition.

So, join me as we delve into the fascinating world of props and embark on a journey that will cultivate a fulfilling and meaningful collection.

Let the adventure begin!

2

The Art and Impact of Prop Significance

The Art and Impact of Prop Significance

In the tapestry of film, television, and theatre, props are silent stalwarts, eloquently adding depth and dimension to tales spun on screen or stage. Far from mere decorative elements, these objects are pivotal in storytelling, character portrayal, and even weaving a cultural legacy. Dive in as we illuminate the profound significance of props in the entertainment cosmos.

1. **Prop as Narratives' Anchor**:
   Visualise the all-time classics – a detective drama devoid of its symbolic magnifying glass or a superhero saga stripped of its signature costume. Props aren't just objects; they're narrative anchors. They set the scene, provide context, and subtly fore-shadow upcoming twists. With deft precision, props stitch the illusion of reality, drawing audiences into the narrative fold.

2. **Character Echoes in Props**:
   Every prop attached to a character is a whisper of their essence.

The habitual coffee mug of a character, for instance, might reveal comforting routines or mask deeper insecurities. Whether it's a journal echoing silent tales or a valiant sword symbolising undying valour, props augment the persona, offering a window into their soul and history.

3. **Prop's Cultural Odyssey:**

Certain props, like Star Wars' lightsaber or The Wizard of Oz's ruby slippers, have evolved beyond cinematic boundaries. They're no longer mere movie accessories but have metamorphosed into cultural insignias, kindling nostalgia, evoking emotions, and becoming emblematic of entire eras.

4. **The Collector's Chronicle:**

For those infatuated with cinematic history, prop collecting is more than a pastime—it's a pilgrimage. For newcomers, it's the thrill of questing for cinematic artefacts, while veterans revel in the joy of preserving the legacy and artistry inherent in these items. Our guide will demystify prop collecting for you, from budgeting nuances to engaging with authentic sellers and understanding valuation.

5. **Crafting Collections:**

Our journey delves deep into prop curation. Garner insights on curating a coherent collection, gauging the value of props, and showcasing them with elegance. Together, we'll also tread the sometimes murky waters of authenticity, arming you with the know-how to differentiate genuine relics from mere replicas.

6. **Power of the Collective:**

While prop collecting can seem an individual pursuit, it thrives on the bedrock of community. Forums, conventions, and gatherings aren't just about transactions; their melting pots of shared passions and collective memories. They offer a space to celebrate cinematic milestones, share stories, and indulge in playful prop competitions.

Props are cinematic keystones. Beyond their on-screen presence, they embody the essence of storytelling, echo character idiosyncrasies, and even etch cultural imprints. They transcend their object-hood, becoming markers of time, emotion, and shared human experiences. Through the lens of this guide, rediscover the enchantment and eloquence of props, these poignant storytellers in their own right.

3

The Thrill of Prop Collecting

The Thrill of Prop Collecting

It's not just about acquiring tangible pieces of our favourite movies, TV shows, or stage productions – it's about owning a little piece of magic. As we delve deeper into the world of prop collecting, we uncover a treasure trove of emotions and experiences that make this hobby so thrilling.

In this chapter, we'll explore the nostalgia factor, the emotional connection we develop with our favourite characters and moments, and why owning props is so much more than just having a physical item.

Unlocking the Time Capsule: Have you ever stumbled upon an old toy, a worn-out comic book, or a beloved movie ticket stub from your childhood? Suddenly, you're transported back in time, reliving those moments of wonder, excitement, and pure joy. That's the power of nostalgia, my friends. And prop collecting takes nostalgia to a whole new level.

Imagine holding Captain America's shield from your favourite Marvel movie or clutching a lightsaber used by Luke Skywalker. These props carry with them the memories and emotions of the characters and stories we hold dear. They become touchstones to the past, allowing us to revisit those magical moments whenever we desire. It's like having a time machine on your shelf!

Emotional Connection: More than just props's aren't just inanimate objects; they are imbued with the essence of the characters and the stories they belong to. When we hold a prop, we can almost feel the presence of our favourite heroes and villains. It's like having a conversation with them, sharing in their triumphs and struggles.

Remember that scene that made you laugh till your sides hurt? Or that heart-wrenching moment that left you in tears?
Owning a prop from that scene is like capturing lightning in a bottle. It's a tangible reminder of the emotional impact these stories have had on us. And when we display these props proudly in our homes, we create a space that reflects our passions and brings us joy every time we walk by.

The bond between fan and prop: Now, let's talk about the magical bond that forms between a fan and their prop. It's like finding a kindred spirit, a companion who understands your love for that particular character or story. When you hold a prop, you feel a connection to the creative minds behind the scenes – the prop makers, the set designers, the actors. It's like joining a secret club, an exclusive community of passionate individuals who share your love for the same fictional worlds.And let's not forget the conversations that come with owning props.

Picture yourself at a dinner party, casually mentioning that you have an authentic Batmobile keychain or a prop wand from Harry Potter. Suddenly, you become the centre of attention, the resident expert on all things pop culture. Your friends will beg you for stories, details, and maybe even a chance to hold these cherished artefacts. You've become a hero in your own right!

The thrill of prop collecting is not just about owning physical items; it's about capturing the intangible magic of our favourite movies, TV shows, and stage productions. It's about preserving memories, connecting with characters, and sharing our love for these stories with the world. So, fellow prop collectors, embrace the excitement and satisfaction that comes from owning props. Let the nostalgia wash over you, forge emotional connections with your favourite characters, and revel in the joy of being a part of this incredible world.

And remember, the best prop collection is the one that brings a smile to your face every single day.

4

Why Collect Props?

Why Collect Props?

The allure of owning a piece of cinematic history!

Have you ever watched a movie and thought, "Wow, I wish I could own that iconic prop"? Well, my fellow prop enthusiasts, you're not alone. The desire to own a piece of cinematic history is a powerful motivator for prop collectors around the world.

Picture this: you're sitting on your couch, popcorn in hand, watching your favourite movie. Suddenly, a prop catches your eye. It could be Harry Potter's wand, Dorothy's ruby slippers, or even Indiana Jones' whip.

In that moment, you feel a connection, a spark of magic. You want to hold that prop, to feel its weight in your hand, and to be transported to the world of your favourite film.

Collecting props allows us to bring the magic of the movies into our own lives. It's like having a little piece of Hollywood right in your living room. You can show off your collection to friends, family, and fellow enthusiasts, impressing them with your cinematic treasures. It's not just about owning an object; it's about owning a piece of the story, a tangible link to the characters and the worlds we love.

But it's not just about the bragging rights. Collecting props is also a way to appreciate the craftsmanship and artistry that goes into creating these iconic objects. Think about it - every prop has been meticulously designed and crafted by skilled artisans. From the intricate details of a superhero's suit to the weathered look of a pirate's treasure map, props are works of art in their own right.

As prop collectors, we become connoisseurs of craftsmanship. We admire the attention to detail, the creativity, and the sheer talent that goes into creating these objects. It's like owning a mini art gallery, with each prop telling a unique story of creativity and ingenuity.

Now, you might be thinking, "Collecting props sounds fun, but isn't it a solitary hobby?" Well, let me introduce you to the vibrant and passionate prop collecting community. Trust me, you'll never feel alone in your love for props again.

Prop collectors are a tight-knit group, brought together by their shared passion for all things cinematic. Whether it's discussing the latest movie releases, swapping stories about their most prized props, or helping each other track down elusive items, the prop collecting community is a supportive and welcoming one.

Think of it as a worldwide fan club, with collectors from all walks of life coming together to celebrate their shared love for the magic of movies.

From online forums and social media groups to conventions and local meet-ups, there are endless opportunities to connect with fellow enthusiasts and build meaningful relationships.Not only can you learn from experienced collectors who are willing to share their wisdom and expertise, but you can also collaborate on projects, trade or sell props, and even attend exclusive events or screenings. The prop collecting community is a treasure trove of knowledge, camaraderie, and friendship.

So, my fellow prop enthusiasts, whether you're motivated by the desire to own a piece of cinematic history, the appreciation for craftsmanship, or the sense of community among collectors, prop collecting is a rewarding and fulfilling journey. It's a way to bring the magic of the movies into your own life, to admire the artistry behind each prop, and to connect with like-minded individuals who share your passion.

In the words of Indiana Jones himself, "It's not the years, honey, it's the mileage."

5

The Impact of Props on Pop Culture

The Impact of Props on Pop Culture

From the golden age of Hollywood to the rise of streaming platforms, props have played a significant role in shaping pop culture as we know it. These seemingly ordinary objects have become iconic symbols, ingrained in the collective memory of audiences worldwide.

Think of the lightsaber from Star Wars, Dorothy's ruby slippers from The Wizard of Oz, or even the iconic white mask worn by Michael Myers in Halloween. These props have transcended their original purpose and have become cultural touchstones, influencing fashion, merchandise, and even fan culture.But how exactly did props become such influential symbols?

It's a fascinating journey that can be traced back to the early days of filmmaking. In the early 20th century, props were simply functional items used to enhance the storytelling process. They served to create a believable and immersive world on screen. However, as audiences began to connect more deeply with the characters and stories they saw, props started to take on a life of their own.

One of the first props to achieve true iconic status was the ruby slippers from The Wizard of Oz. These sparkly red shoes not only captured the imagination of audiences but also became a symbol of empowerment for many. Dorothy's journey through the fantastical land of Oz resonated with viewers, and the shoes represented her determination and resilience. It wasn't long before the ruby slippers became a sought-after item, with fans eager to own a piece of cinematic history.This trend continued to grow over the years, with props from various movies and TV shows capturing the hearts of fans. Take the DeLorean time machine from Back to the Future, for example.

This iconic vehicle, complete with its flux capacitor and gull-wing doors, has become synonymous with time travel and adventure. Fans of the franchise have even gone so far as to recreate their own DeLorean replicas, showcasing the enduring impact of this prop on pop culture.

The influence of props on fashion cannot be overlooked either. From the sleek, black sunglasses worn by the Men in Black to the cow-print jacket sported by Marty McFly in Back to the Future, props have inspired countless fashion trends. Designers often draw inspiration from these iconic objects, incorporating elements into their collections and creating a sense of nostalgia for fans.

In addition to fashion, props have also had a profound impact on merchandise. Who can forget the plethora of Star Wars action figures, lightsaber replicas, and Death Star Lego sets? These items allow fans to take a piece of their favourite movies or TV shows home with them, further deepening their connection to the stories and characters they love.But perhaps one of the most significant impacts of props on pop culture is the rise of fan culture. Fans have always been passionate about their favourite movies and TV shows, but props have provided a tangible way for them to express their love and dedication. From cosplay conventions to fan-made prop replicas, enthusiasts have found creative ways to immerse themselves in the worlds they adore. The shared experience of appreciating and collecting props has brought fans together, forming communities and fostering a sense of belonging.

Props have become more than just inanimate objects in the world of entertainment. They have become powerful symbols that shape and define pop culture. From influencing fashion trends to inspiring merchandise and fan culture, these props have left an indelible mark on society. So the next time you watch a movie or TV show, take a moment to appreciate the props that bring these stories to life. Who knows, you might just discover a new passion for collecting these iconic symbols of pop culture. And remember, if you ever come across a lightsaber or a pair of ruby slippers, seize the opportunity.

After all, who wouldn't want to own a piece of cinematic magic?

6

———

The Evolution of Prop Collecting

The Evolution of Prop Collecting

Tracing the Journey of Prop Collecting: From Niche Passion to Esteemed Pursuit

Imagine a scene: you're nestled in your favourite armchair, encircled by an array of iconic props from the movies and TV shows that have left an indelible mark on your life. As you cast your eyes upon these treasures, an overwhelming sense of awe and wonder fills the room. Each prop, each artefact, encapsulates a slice of cinematic history – a tangible link to the characters and narratives that have shaped our collective imagination. This is the realm of prop collecting, a journey that has gracefully evolved from its humble origins into a dynamic and respected endeavour.

In its nascent stages, prop collecting existed as a niche and little-known pursuit. It was birthed by a handful of fervent individuals who recognised the intrinsic value of preserving and savouring these tangible relics from the realm of entertainment. Their collections began as modest assortments, procured through personal contacts or serendipitous encounters. But as word spread and fervour grew, prop collecting underwent a transformation, birthing a burgeoning community of enthusiasts.

The Resurgence of the Blockbuster Prop: The inception of blockbuster films in the 1970s and 1980s catalysed the meteoric rise of prop collecting. Suddenly, the allure of props from iconic franchises like Star Wars and Indiana Jones became irresistible. These once-utilitarian objects, now imbued with profound emotional and monetary worth, ignited a feverish demand. Collectors scrambled to lay claim to lightsabers, fedoras, and other emblematic relics from their adored cinematic sagas. The epoch of prop collecting had arrived in full splendour.

From Pastime to Investment Avenue: With the passage of time, prop collecting transcended its role as a mere pastime. What began as a pursuit fuelled by sentiment and nostalgia eventually drew the attention of investors and speculators. The revelation that these props held potential as viable investment opportunities instigated a palpable enthusiasm within the community. Objects that were formerly curiosities underwent a renaissance, as they emerged as potential appreciating assets, enticing those seeking to diversify their investment portfolios.

The Digital Era and the Dawn of Replica Prop Collecting: The advent of the internet ushered prop collecting into a novel epoch. Virtual domains and online communities dedicated to this art form flourished, serving as global congregations for collectors. This digital age also witnessed the emergence of a novel facet within prop collecting: the realm of replica props. Meticulously fashioned replicas granted enthusiasts the chance to possess items closely mirroring their authentic counterparts, regardless of budget limitations. The practice of collecting replica props burgeoned into a vibrant subculture within the broader prop collecting landscape.

Pioneering the Tomorrow of Prop Collecting: As the trajectory of prop collecting continues its evolution, a singular certainty prevails: the ardor and ardency of collectors will steadfastly endure. The horizon holds tantalising prospects, from innovations in replica prop fabrication to the unearthing of forgotten treasures languishing within obscured storehouses. With fresh cinematic narratives captivating imaginations, a new generation of prop collectors will invariably emerge, ensuring the vitality and perpetuity of this cherished pursuit.

The voyage of prop collecting has traversed a considerable expanse from its unassuming origins. What once existed as a niche preoccupation, cherished by a select few, has blossomed into a global phenomenon. The evolution of prop collecting mirrors our own odyssey through our adoration for films, television, and the enchanting universe of entertainment. As we persist in commemorating the stories and personas that have left an indelible imprint on our hearts, prop collecting serves as a venerated conduit to forge connections with these revered works of art.

So, whether you're a neophyte collector embarking on your inaugural odyssey or a seasoned devotee with an array of cherished props, remember this: each prop encapsulates a narrative, and every narrative merits safeguarding and reverence. Who knows? Someday, you might find yourself in the congenial company of fellow prop enthusiasts, swapping anecdotes and laughter over libations, while marvelling at the enchanting evolution of prop collecting. For, truly, what finer way to invest your time than by immersing yourself in the magic of cinema, one prop at a time?

A timeline of the history:

The evolution of prop collecting has an interesting history that spans several decades. While the practice of collecting items related to entertainment can be traced back to the early days of film and theatre, the organised collecting of movie and TV show props gained significant traction in the latter half of the 20th century. Here's a brief overview of the evolution of prop collecting:

Early Years:

- **Golden Age of Hollywood:** During the early days of Hollywood, many movie studios didn't place a high value on preserving props and costumes. As a result, numerous items were discarded or repurposed, making surviving props from this era rare and valuable collector's items today.

1960s - 1970s:

- **Emergence of Fandom:** The rise of fan conventions and the growth of organised fandom during the 1960s and 1970s led to increased interest in collecting items related to favourite movies and TV shows.

- **Famous Auctions:** High-profile auctions, such as the MGM auction in 1970, which included items from classics like "The Wizard of Oz," brought attention to the idea of owning pieces of cinematic history.

1980s - 1990s:

- **Star Wars Craze:** The popularity of franchises like "Star Wars" in the late 1970s and early 1980s ignited a fervour for collecting memorabilia, including props and action figures.

- **Growing Market:** As VHS tapes and cable television became more common, fans had increased access to their favourite movies and TV shows, fuelling a desire for related collectibles.

- **Convention Culture:** Sci-fi and comic book conventions provided platforms for fans to buy, sell, and trade memorabilia, including props.

2000s - Present:

- **Internet Revolution:** The proliferation of the internet and online marketplaces made it easier for collectors to connect, trade, and purchase items. Specialist websites dedicated to prop collecting also emerged.

- **Authenticity and Documentation:** Collectors became more focused on the authenticity of items, leading to a greater demand for provenance and certificates of authenticity (COAs).

- **Auction Houses:** Reputable auction houses started hosting dedicated entertainment memorabilia auctions, showcasing rare and valuable props.

- **Increased Mainstream Interest:** The success of pop culture conventions like San Diego Comic-Con and the growth of fan communities contributed to the mainstream acceptance of prop collecting.

- **Higher Values:** As the rarity of certain items increased, so did their monetary value. Some iconic props have sold for significant sums in auctions.

- **Cultural Impact:** Collecting has become a cultural phenomenon, with TV shows like "Pawn Stars" and "Hollywood Treasure" featuring stories of prop collectors and their acquisitions.

Overall, the evolution of prop collecting reflects the changing dynamics of media consumption, fan engagement, and the increasing recognition of entertainment memorabilia as valuable cultural artefacts. The journey from humble beginnings to the modern collector's market is marked by the passion of enthusiasts and the preservation of the stories behind the props that have shaped our favourite movies and TV shows.

Here's to the props that infuse delight into our lives and the stories they narrate.

7

Getting Started

Getting Started

Setting Collecting Goals: Your Voyage into Prop Collecting Excellence

Embarking on the journey of prop collecting requires a compass to guide you through the intricate waters of this captivating pursuit. Crafting well-defined collecting goals stands as the foundation of this endeavour, lending purpose, precision, and fulfilment to your odyssey. Whether your heart longs to possess relics from specific movies, TV shows, or genres, or desires to assemble an eclectic collection encapsulating the vast spectrum of entertainment, the art of setting goals will illuminate your path and transform your experience.

Navigating the First Steps:

Begin by carving out a moment of reflection. What ignites your fervour for prop collecting? Is it the thrill of grasping a tangible piece of your treasured movie's legacy? Or perhaps the allure of curating a collection that narrates its own cinematic saga? Maybe it's the intricate craftsmanship that molds these iconic pieces. Unearth your motivations, for they will be the building blocks of your goals.

Focusing the Telescope:

Having unveiled your driving force, let's delve into specificity. What facet of props or memorabilia stirs the embers of your passion? Do you revel in the galaxies of Star Wars, yearning for lightsabers and droids to grace your collection? Or does the macabre allure of horror beckon, enticing you with eerie artefacts that tingle your spine? Delineating your focus not only elevates your collecting voyage but also simplifies your search and facilitates connections with fellow enthusiasts.

Budgeting the Horizon:

Before the enthusiasm sails too far, anchor in reality. Contemplate your budget. Prop collecting can be an investment, and prudence is vital. Define your financial boundaries. A budget will steer your acquisitions and protect you from being swept into an unending quest for the unattainable Holy Grail prop. Remember, value rests in quality, not quantity. Cherish a collection that evokes genuine sentiment, foregoing a profusion of items that languish on shelves, forgotten.

Unleashing the Imaginary:

Now, let's introduce a dash of whimsy to this maritime voyage. Imagine standing amid a room festooned with props from your beloved cinematic masterpieces. Your collection is a splendid tapestry weaving together an eclectic variety, akin to an intergalactic cantina's buffet. From lightsabers of Star Wars to wands of Harry Potter, the narrative threads are as diverse as the colours of a rainbow. Here's the kicker: prop collecting transcends mere artefacts. It encompasses the stories woven, the memories invoked. Thus, craft goals that surpass the physical; delve into the emotional fabric. Envision how your collection should resonate. A nostalgic time machine? A creative catalyst?

Tailor your emotional aspirations for a collection that delights, uplifts, and resonates within.

Sailing Forward with Purpose:

Setting collecting goals is akin to charting a course through uncharted waters. It defines your intent, harnesses your ardor, and propels you through the boundless realm of props, armed with assurance and exhilaration.

Embrace your inner cartographer (or spreadsheet guru) as you plot your goals. Be meticulous in specificity, considerate of your budget, and poignant in the emotional tapestry you intend to weave. Relish every moment, for prop collecting is a journey, meant to be savoured.

8

Budgeting for Prop Collecting

Budgeting for Prop Collecting

Mastering the Art of Budgeting for Prop Collecting:

Diving into the realm of prop collecting is akin to stepping into a treasure trove of cinematic history. It's a thrilling endeavour that allows aficionados to immerse themselves in the very essence of their favourite movies, TV shows, and video games. However, just like any passionate pursuit, successful prop collecting demands prudent budgeting to ensure the growth of your collection without causing financial strain. In this segment, we will delve into strategic and pragmatic advice on budgeting for prop collecting, covering an array of facets, from saving strategies to the preservation of your cherished pieces.

1. **Crafting the Foundation: Saving for Prop Collecting**

   Before you embark on your prop collecting odyssey, laying a sturdy financial foundation is paramount. This begins with establishing a dedicated budget and saving regimen. Devote a specific percentage of your monthly income exclusively to prop collecting. By allocating funds this way, you ensure that your everyday finances remain unaffected while you indulge your passion. Automating this savings process can be a shrewd move – set up automatic transfers to a separate account earmarked solely for your prop collecting ventures.

2. **Strategic Acquisitions: Prioritising Purchases**

   In the realm of prop collecting, the landscape is vast and teeming with options. To navigate it astutely, prioritise your purchases. Identify the particular niches within prop collecting that resonate most with you and allocate a portion of your budget toward these focal points. This strategic approach circumvents impulsive spending, allowing you to acquire items that genuinely elevate your collection and bring you profound joy.

3. **The Pillar of Authenticity: Research and Authentication**

   Ensuring the authenticity of your acquisitions is pivotal in prop collecting. Dedicate a segment of your budget to authentication services to validate the legitimacy of your coveted props. Conduct comprehensive research to identify reputable authentication experts or organisations. Authenticated props hold enduring value and appreciation over time, making this allocation a judicious investment in the future of your collection.

4. **Safeguarding the Legacy: Preservation and Maintenance**

   Preserving the integrity of your prop collection is non-negotiable. Allocate funds within your budget for safeguarding measures. This encompasses appropriate storage solutions, display cases, and protective materials like archival packaging or climate-controlled environments. By prioritising preservation, you shield your props from potential deterioration, ensuring their value remains intact for years to come.

5. **Harnessing Modern Tools: Budgeting Apps and Resources**

Leveraging the technological advancements of today, embrace budgeting tools and apps to streamline your prop collecting financials. These resources offer insights into your spending habits, facilitate goal-setting, and aid in tracking your expenses. Analysing these patterns empowers you to identify potential areas for savings or re-allocation of funds toward your prop collecting passion.

Budgeting for prop collecting is a strategic art that marries your fervour for collecting with fiscal responsibility. By committing to consistent saving, strategising purchases, earmarking funds for authentication and preservation, and utilising cutting-edge budgeting tools, you ensure your prop collecting journey is not just sustainable, but deeply rewarding. Remember, the essence lies in striking an equilibrium between indulging in your passion and nurturing your financial health.

Your collection is more than just an assemblage of items; it's a testament to your appreciation for the art of storytelling.

9

Establishing a collection plan

Establishing a collection plan

Crafting Your Prop Collecting Focus: A Navigator's Guide

The decision to voyage into this captivating world is commendable. However, before you set sail and adorn your shelves with an eclectic assortment of items spanning diverse movies, TV shows, and eras, there's a pivotal step to consider: choosing a collection focus. Think of it as the North Star that will illuminate your course through the expansive galaxy of prop possibilities.

Crafting a collection focus offers more than mere coherence; it's your compass to traverse this vast terrain with purpose. This thoughtful selection streamlines your search and concentrates your efforts on acquiring pieces that resonate with your passion. After all, a collection adorned with unrelated miscellany isn't the goal. Let's embark on a journey to discover the methods of pinpointing your collection focus, elevating your prop collecting voyage to new heights.

Steering by Stars:

One approach is to turn your gaze towards your favourite actors, directors, or historical eras. Are you a fervent admirer of Tom Hanks? Delve into collecting props from his iconic films like "Forrest Gump" or "Cast Away." If the golden age of Hollywood beckons, perhaps your collection will feature treasures from timeless classics such as "Gone with the Wind" or "Casablanca." This method weaves a thematic thread through your collection, intertwining it with your personal interests and inclinations.

Blueprints of Interest:

Another avenue involves pondering the type of props that kindle your imagination. Are your curiosities drawn to costumes, weapons, or the intricate minutiae of vehicles? Do the intricate set designs or meticulously crafted props that breathe life into fictional universes captivate you? By identifying the very essence of what captures your fascination, you can decisively streamline your focus and commence crafting a collection that mirrors your passions.

Unleashing Creative Boundaries:

Don't hesitate to infuse creativity into your collection focus. Perhaps your desire is to accumulate props from a specific genre, like the realms of sci-fi or fantasy. Alternatively, your aspiration might involve acquiring items from resplendent stage productions or ballet performances. The horizons are boundless. The pivotal aspect is to select a focus that ignites not only your enthusiasm but also your inquisitiveness, as this zeal will propel your prop collecting odyssey.

Mastering Budget Navigation:

Budget is the companion that mustn't be overlooked. When establishing your collection focus, align it with your financial parameters. Certain props may arrive with substantial price tags, particularly if they hail from cherished movies or are in high demand among collectors. Hence, crafting a budget that resonates with your fiscal reality is vital. Remember, prop collecting is akin to a marathon, allowing you to expand your collection gradually as your financial capacity evolves.

As you embark on this prop collecting odyssey, embrace the fact that your collection focus can evolve organically over time. A journey that commences with collecting props from a beloved actor's filmography may organically branch out to encompass diverse eras and genres. The essence lies in staying true to your passions and permitting your collection to blossom naturally.

Remember, the choice of a collection focus is merely the commencement of your prop collecting odyssey.

10

Embarking on Your Prop Collecting Journey: Starting Small with Beginner's Tips

Embarking on Your Prop Collecting Journey: Starting Small with Beginner's Tips

You've taken those initial steps into the captivating realm of prop collecting, venturing into the world of affordable treasures that have kindled a spark within you. Now, as you stand at the precipice of progress, your desire to dive deeper grows stronger. You're ready to delve into the prop collecting community, to forge connections with fellow enthusiasts, and to expand your collection with items that hold even greater sentimental value. Your aspirations are commendable, and your timing is impeccable. In this chapter, we shall delve into the enchanting expanse of local events and networking, a realm where prop collecting possibilities await in abundance.

Navigating the Enchanted Realm of Local Events:

Picture yourself stepping through the threshold of local events; it's akin to entering a hidden sanctum of prop collecting enchantment. Be it a convention, a fan meet-up, or a prop auction, these gatherings are more than mere occasions; they are hubs teeming with exhilaration, camaraderie, and, naturally, a plethora of enticing props. So, don your metaphorical prop-hunting hat, slip into your most comfortable footwear, and let's embark on a journey through the myriad wonders awaiting your discovery.

The Marvels of Conventions:

Conventions, those dynamic congregations of kindred spirits who share your zeal for cinema and television marvels, offer an array of prop-related activities. Workshops, panels, and the coveted chance to engage with specialised prop vendors await. Here, you'll find an assortment of treasures, from iconic film weaponry to costumes donned by beloved characters. It's a prop collector's reverie materialised.

As you traverse the convention floor, invest time in conversations with vendors and fellow collectors. Exchange inquiries, share narratives, and absorb wisdom like a sponge. You might uncover hidden gems or gain invaluable insights. Moreover, forming bonds with like-minded enthusiasts enriches the experience. Remember, prop collecting transcends the artefacts; it's the friendships and memories that endure.

Unveiling the Allure of Local Prop Auctions:

For those unenthused by conventions or without access to them, local prop auctions stand as an equally enthralling avenue. These gatherings unite prop aficionados, collectors, and occasionally even creators. Picture yourself within the dimly lit ambiance of an auction hall, pulse racing, as the auctioneer's voice crescendos with each bid for the prop that has captivated your attention all evening. The rush of adrenaline is unparalleled. And should fortune favour your endeavour, you might depart with a fragment of cinematic history in hand.

Beyond Treasures: Networking and Connections:

Attending local events is a gateway not solely to expanding your collection but also to unearthing new prospects and knowledge. The encounters you make might lead to serendipitous finds or offer insights during workshops conducted by industry experts on prop preservation. These occasions brim with wisdom-sharing, and the prevailing enthusiasm makes every conversation valuable.

Yet, the voyage extends beyond the physical realm of events. Networking with fellow collectors forms an integral facet. Engaging in online forums, social media groups, or local meet-ups creates connections with those who share your passion. This network transforms into a foundation of support, a space to discuss recent acquisitions or seek guidance when authenticity is uncertain.

Your Journey of Prop Collecting Awaits:

Let the thrill and allure of local events and networking infuse your prop collecting journey. Submerge yourself within this captivating community, enrich your understanding, and observe your collection flourish. Remember, no collection is too diminutive for a humble beginning, and no novice enthusiast stands separate from the ranks of seasoned collectors. The road is yours to navigate, and the treasures are waiting to be uncovered.

11

Unveiling the Tales Behind Movie Props: A Guide to Researching Prop History

Unveiling the Tales Behind Movie Props: A Guide to Researching Prop History

For aficionados of movie prop collecting, it's universally acknowledged that the allure isn't limited to simply possessing the artefact. In fact, the deeper thrill often comes from deciphering the prop's unique tale. The narrative behind a prop can be as riveting as the artifact itself, and venturing into its history can augment your appreciation manifold. In this guide, we delve into the intricate process of researching prop history and offer insights into the most valuable resources at your disposal.

Starting Your Quest: Once a prop captivates your attention, the journey to unearth its background begins. Thankfully, the digital age grants us vast platforms for research. Esteemed websites like Prop Store, Heritage Auctions, and Profiles in History house comprehensive archives detailing the lineage and significance of props. These platforms often shine a spotlight on expert interviews and insider stories, offering rare glimpses into the world of prop lore.

The Timelessness of Books: Don't be swayed solely by the convenience of the digital world. Books, such as "The Art of the Movie Prop" and "Hollywood Collectibles," can be a goldmine for prop enthusiasts. Packed with visually arresting images and firsthand narratives from industry stalwarts, they illuminate the role of props in the tapestry of cinematic narratives.

Documenting the Details: Streaming platforms like Netflix and Amazon Prime are home to an array of documentaries that pull back the curtain on filmmaking and prop creation. Gems like "The Propmasters" and "Artifact" offer immersive experiences into the craftsmanship and passion driving prop creation.

Conversations with Connoisseurs: To venture beyond documented tales, consider interacting with the experts directly. Candid conversations with prop collectors, production artisans, and actors privy to prop-related anecdotes can be a treasure trove. Their firsthand accounts often weave a tapestry of details, lending context to a prop's cinematic presence and sharing tales rarely documented elsewhere.

Community Chronicles: The prop collector community is an expansive network of knowledge. Dive into online forums, join social media circles, or immerse yourself in prop conventions. These spaces resonate with shared experiences, tips, and resources, enriching your research journey.

The Power of Inquiry: Never hesitate to pose questions. Whether you're interviewing an expert or connecting with a fellow enthusiast, approach with an inquisitive mind. Inquiries about a prop's origin, its cinematic journey, or associated trivia can uncover nuanced details, enhancing the richness of your collection.

In essence, prop collecting is akin to a detective's pursuit: unraveling enigmas and uncovering the unanticipated. Armed with an array of resources—ranging from online repositories and literary treasures to documentaries and personal narratives—you're equipped to unveil the compelling chronicles ensconced within your props.

Approach with an unyielding curiosity, engage actively with the community, and relish every quirk and revelation. Here's to transformative discoveries!

12

Mastering Prop Authenticity: A Collector's Guide

Mastering Prop Authenticity: A Collector's Guide

In the realm of prop collecting, there's an art to ensuring what you acquire is genuine. After all, the pride in showcasing a prop is diminished if it's merely a replica or worse, an outright counterfeit. As we step into the intricate world of prop authenticity, let's unravel the determinants that certify a prop's genuineness.

1. **Understanding Provenance**: Think of provenance as a prop's historical ledger. It traces the prop's lineage and its passage through time. The strength and clarity of this documentation often correlate with the authenticity of the item. A well-documented provenance is your prop's strongest ally. In essence, always trust the paper trail!

2.

3. **Decoding Production Materials**: Imagine believing you've obtained a genuine prop, only to discern it's made from an inferior material. Authentic props are often birthed from materials synonymous with the original production. Any deviation in material quality can be a telltale sign of inauthenticity. Be vigilant and discerning in your assessments!

4.

5. **Studio Markings: The Hidden Authenticators**: These often-subtle imprints, be it logos or serial numbers, act as silent validators of a prop's origin. Tucked away in covert corners or behind panels, they are veritable proofs of a studio's craftsmanship. Engage in a detective-esque search for these markings; they're your assurance of authenticity.

6.

7. **Navigating the World of Replicas**: It's vital to remember that the prop collecting domain isn't devoid of doppelgangers. Some replicas are crafted with such finesse they can deceive even the most seasoned eyes. However, with keen attention to detail—be it in craftsmanship, material consistency, or prop dimensions—you can discern the genuine from the faux. Moreover, exercise caution when a deal appears overly generous; if it sounds too good to be true, it likely is!

In summary, prop collecting is a tantalising dance of observation and knowledge. Provenance, production materials, and studio markings collectively weave the fabric of a prop's authenticity. Your astute eye and discernment play an invaluable role in differentiating genuine treasures from mere imitations.

13

The Elegance of Prop Collecting: An Insight into Rarity and Value

The Elegance of Prop Collecting: An Insight into Rarity and Value

In the mesmerising realm of films and TV shows, have you ever been captivated by a specific prop, desiring to hold a fragment of that cinematic magic? If so, you tread a path many enthusiasts have walked. But as with any treasure hunt, discerning the truly rare gems from the ordinary is an art in itself. Here's your guide to identifying and acquiring the crème de la crème of the prop world.

1. **Limited Edition Props – The Crown Jewels:**

   These are the prop world's equivalent to limited edition artworks. Designed in restricted numbers, they inherently possess rarity. A certificate of authenticity often accompanies such treasures, amplifying their worth. Be it action figures, costumes, or replicas, the exclusivity of limited editions makes them a collector's dream. So, during your prop expeditions, be on the lookout for signs indicating their limited nature.

2. **Screen-Used Items – Direct Lineage to Stardom**:

   Nothing screams authenticity like props that have graced the screen. These items, having shared space with actors, are steeped in the aura of the film or show they come from. To identify such rarities, delve deep. Seek behind-the-scenes footage, interviews, or documentation mentioning prop usage. Screen-worn signs, such as distinctive marks or wear patterns, can be indicative of their authenticity.

3. **Props of Historical or Sentimental Import**:

   Beyond their physical presence, some props resonate profoundly due to their historical or emotional significance. A prop from a cinematic milestone or a beloved series that marked an era holds unparalleled appeal. Their ability to evoke memories and nostalgia amplifies their desirability and value.

4. **The Quest for the Quintessential Prop**:

   Your quest for these cinematic treasures commences online. Platforms like Prop Store, ScreenUsed, and Profiles in History are excellent starting points. Esteemed auction houses, such as Sotheby's and Christie's, occasionally spotlight cinematic props. Furthermore, events like Comic-cons or fan expos can be goldmines, offering diverse arrays from replicas to genuine screen-used marvels. However, a word to the wise: always vet the item's authenticity and the seller's credibility.

5. **Appraising Prop Value**:

While assessing a prop's worth, myriad factors come into play—demand, condition, its backstory, and more. Continual education about the prop market, expert consultations, and trend awareness are vital. Yet, beyond the fiscal worth, it's pivotal to remember the intangible value these items carry: the joy, nostalgia, and connectivity to cinematic artistry.

As you add to your collection, each prop, whether renowned for its rarity, screen presence, or profound sentiment, becomes a storyteller, echoing tales of cinematic brilliance.

14

Online Prop Marketplaces

Online Prop Marketplaces

The advent of the digital era has truly redefined the prop collecting landscape. With the power of the internet, iconic props from celebrated movies, enthralling TV shows, and captivating stage productions are now just a few clicks away. Enter the dynamic domain of online prop marketplaces!

These platforms have emerged as invaluable assets for collectors, presenting an expansive spectrum of items, from legendary movie props to singular artefacts from theatrical shows. However, the vastness of the digital space requires careful navigation. Below, we spotlight prominent online prop platforms, outlining their advantages, potential pitfalls, security considerations, and strategies to identify trustworthy sellers.

Prop Store stands as a dominant player in this realm. Catering to an international audience, it boasts an impressive inventory of props, costumes, and production-related memorabilia. While the platform wins accolades for its diverse offerings and stringent authentication processes, collectors should be prepared for potentially high price points. It's imperative to set financial parameters to ensure a fulfilling buying experience.

eBay offers another extensive marketplace but demands additional vigilance. Given its non-specialised nature, ensuring authenticity is paramount. Prospective buyers should meticulously examine seller feedback, demand comprehensive item descriptions, and insist on transparent imagery. As the adage goes, if it appears too good to be true, tread carefully.

The **Replica Props Forum (RPF)**, tailored explicitly for prop aficionados, fosters an engaged community. The forum's layout allows for direct dialogues with sellers and fosters camaraderie amongst enthusiasts. However, since RPF operates on peer-to-peer inter-actions, thorough due diligence is essential.

Safety remains paramount. Collectors should insist on detailed prop provenance and, when feasible, request authenticity certificates. Many top-tier platforms incorporate rigorous seller vetting pro-cedures, augmenting transactional security.

Identifying reputable sellers is streamlined by examining customer feedback and maintaining active participation in online prop collect-ing forums.

Prop collecting transcends mere acquisition; it's a journey into cinematic universes. While online platforms provide unparalleled access, it's essential to navigate them with knowledge, caution, and an insatiable passion.

Auction House Prop Sales

Delving into auction house prop sales is akin to venturing into an exhilarating cinematic universe. From the methodical research phase to the electric atmosphere of live bidding, the entire journey is drenched in anticipation and thrill.

Research is the cornerstone. Fledgling and seasoned collectors alike should meticulously scan auction listings, gauging market temperature, and item valuations. Aligning with reputable auction houses ensures transactional authenticity. Seeking insights from seasoned collectors and participating in dedicated forums can be enlightening.

Establishing budgetary boundaries is critical. In the whirlwind of bidding wars, a pre-set limit serves as a grounding anchor. It's about balancing passion with prudence.

Understanding the auction dynamics is equally vital. Familiarise yourself with registration prerequisites, incremental bidding structures, and any ancillary fees.

On the auction day, channel calmness. While the environment pulsates with excitement, maintaining composure aids rational decision-making. Celebrate the wins, learn from the losses, and immerse yourself in the grand tapestry of stories each prop narrates.

Embrace the auction world with informed enthusiasm, letting each bid draw you closer to cinematic masterpieces.

Visiting Prop Shops and Conventions

The digital age, while offering convenience, cannot replicate the tangible magic of physical prop shops and conventions. It's an immersive universe where every corner turned unravels a surprise, and every conversation struck potentially opens doors to a treasure trove.

Prop shops are akin to Aladdin's cave—filled with myriad wonders from various entertainment eras. Beyond mere acquisitions, they offer stories, nostalgia, and a tactile connection to entertainment history.

Conventions, meanwhile, are festivals of fandoms. With stalls brimming with unique artefacts and attendees donning intricate cosplays, the energy is palpable. Beyond purchases, conventions are networking hubs, fostering connections and friendships bound by shared passions.

Both avenues present collectors with the unique joy of discovery, stories of artistry, and the shared camaraderie of like-minded enthusiasts. So, whether you're initiating your prop journey or are a seasoned collector, physical exploration offers a rich tapestry of experiences that promise to be unforgettable.

Acquiring Props Directly From The Source: Production Companies

For the discerning prop collector, there's a certain unparalleled allure in securing pieces directly from their genesis: the production companies. This means acquiring a tangible shard of cinematic or television history, devoid of intermediaries. In essence, it's like plucking a gem right from the treasure chest of a beloved show or film. If the idea of such direct procurement excites you, let's delve into the intricacies of direct sales from production companies.

1. **Starting the Hunt:** Your first mission involves tracking down studio archives or their prop departments. While this might sound daunting, in today's digital era, a strategic online search can typically point you towards the relevant contacts.

2. **The Art of Approach:** After zeroing in on the right channels, it's pivotal to ensure your first impression is memorable. Remember, production houses are bustling hubs. So, ensure your communication is courteous, succinct, and demonstrates genuine interest. Delving into specific movies or series that resonate with you could make your appeal more heartfelt and relatable.

3. **Crafting the Proposal:** Should you strike gold and the company is open to selling, they may require a detailed proposal. This is your canvas – paint a vivid picture of your passion. Elaborate on the prop's significance to you, your plans for its display, and your commitment to its preservation. Let this be a testimony to your fervour!

4. **Navigating the Landscape:** While the idea of direct sales is exhilarating, remember that not all production companies indulge in this practice. If faced with a dead-end, exhibit pro-

activeness. Ask them for recommendations, like affiliated prop shops or auction houses. Many doors lead to paradise, after all.

5. **The Price Spectrum:** Like all good things, exquisite props come at a cost. Direct sales can oscillate considerably in price, contingent on the prop's prominence, scarcity, and overall demand. It's always prudent to have a ballpark figure in mind and broach the subject of pricing early on.

6. **Legal Labyrinth:** Venturing into direct sales can sometimes be coupled with legal intricacies like licensing clauses, intellectual property considerations, or copyright constraints. It's essential to be well-acquainted with these facets. Remember, our aim is treasuring artefacts, not trespassing boundaries!

To encapsulate, acquiring props straight from production companies offers an exhilarating avenue to elevate your collection. This journey is not just about the acquisition but also about the story, the chase, and the cherished connections. Here's to adding not just props, but stories to your collection!

15

Guide to Evaluating Prop Sellers

Guide to Evaluating Prop Sellers

In the intriguing realm of prop collecting, discernment is key. Much like curating a fine art collection, one must approach prop acquisitions with a meticulous eye, ensuring each piece's authenticity and its seller's credibility. As you navigate this niche market, here's a comprehensive guide to help you adeptly evaluate prop sellers and curate a collection worthy of applause.

1. **Prioritise Reputation:** The first checkpoint is the seller's standing within the community. Are they consistently lauded for transparency and authenticity? Does their portfolio exude a legacy of genuine transactions? Conversely, are there any whispers or outright accusations against them? Given that the prop collecting community thrives on word-of-mouth, always be attuned to feedback, whether it resembles a blockbuster's rave reviews or its harsh criticisms.

2. **Demand Documentation:** A genuine seller knows the value of documentation. Request verification papers like Certificates of Authenticity (COA) or associated provenance. These are not just papers but a seal of trust. Be wary of sellers who evade such requests; no one wants a prop reminiscent of a movie's CGI – flashy yet inauthentic.

3. **Ensure Transaction Security:** Beyond the prop's authenticity, ensure your financial transactions are shielded. Opt for established payment gateways, like PayPal or credible escrow services. Remember, just as in a cinematic espionage, here too, safeguarding your assets is paramount.

4. **Communication is King:** A seller's responsiveness can often mirror their credibility. How swiftly do they address queries? Is there a genuine effort to assuage concerns? The key to any successful deal, akin to a movie's gripping dialogue, lies in clear, transparent communication.

5. **Harness Your Intuition:** Sometimes, the cues lie beyond reviews or documents. If a deal feels sketchy or unrealistically perfect, pause. Tune into your instincts. In the world of prop collecting, channeling your inner sleuth isn't just fanciful; it's essential. Adopt the motto: "Trust, but validate."

6. **Network and Connect:** Often, longstanding collectors or enthusiasts can offer invaluable insights. They've been down this road and can provide recommendations or warnings based on firsthand experiences. Consider joining forums or collector groups to tap into this reservoir of knowledge.

7. **Enjoy the Journey:** At its core, prop collecting is a journey of passion, discovery, and narratives. As you add each piece, you're not just collecting objects but fragments of cinematic history. Relish this experience, learn from the twists, and let each acquisition be a cherished chapter in your prop collecting saga.

Tread the world of prop collecting with a blend of excitement, caution, and knowledge. Like any movie buff knows, every detail counts. By meticulously vetting sellers and adhering to this guide, you're set to be the discerning director of your prop collection, ensuring each acquisition is nothing short of a blockbuster.

16

Mastering the Art of Displaying and Storing Collectible Props

Mastering the Art of Displaying and Storing Collectible Props

Dive into the world of prop collecting, and you'll quickly realise that acquisition is just half the journey. The way you showcase and store your coveted treasures speaks volumes about your appreciation for these unique artefacts. After all, every prop has its story, and it deserves to be told with the reverence it commands. So, whether you're new to this realm or seeking to refine your setup, let's delve into the nuances of curating an exquisite display and ensuring longevity for your collectibles.

1. **Curated Presentation:** Think of your display area as a miniature museum. Your props are not mere objects but exhibits that narrate tales of cinematic adventures. Match the aesthetics of your display case to the essence of your collection. A sleek,

modern case might suit contemporary movie props, while an ornate, vintage cabinet may better complement classic film artefacts.

2. **Guard Against the Elements:** Protecting your props from environmental hazards is paramount. Humidity, sunlight, and dust are arch-nemeses. Consider UV-protective glass for display cases in sunlit rooms, and perhaps invest in dehumidifiers if moisture is a concern. For delicate items like manuscripts or costume fabrics, archival-quality sleeves or acid-free tissue paper offer an added layer of protection.

3. **Light it Up:** Ambient lighting can make all the difference. LED lights, being cooler and energy-efficient, are perfect for emphasising particular pieces without risking damage. Spotlights can add dramatic flair, turning your prop into an undeniable conversation starter.

4. **Cohesive Storytelling:** When arranging your props, aim for thematic cohesion. Group items that hail from the same movie, genre, or era. This visual storytelling can breathe life into your collection, allowing viewers to traverse through various cinematic epochs.

5. **Safe Storage:** As your prop family expands, not every member might find a spot in the limelight. For these cherished items in storage, sturdy boxes with custom foam inserts can be a good solution, preventing movement and possible damage. Keep an inventory list and label storage containers; this way, each prop is readily accessible when its time to shine arrives.

6. **Routine Maintenance:** Even props at rest demand care. Periodic dusting, gentle cleaning, and a vigilant eye for signs of wear or deterioration can maintain their value and integrity. With regular attention, your props can remain in impeccable condition, just like a classic film that never fades.

7. **Community Engagement:** Your collection is a reflection of your passion. Why not invite fellow enthusiasts for a viewing?

Sharing insights, stories, and perhaps a hint of friendly envy can build lasting bonds. Organising themed nights or even virtual tours of your collection could be a delightful endeavour.

In Retrospect: The journey of prop collecting is as much about cherishing the past as it is about ensuring a legacy for the future. By curating, safeguarding, and narrating the stories of your props, you're not just a collector – you're a custodian of cinematic history. Celebrate every prop, narrate its lore, and remember, every spotlight you cast adds a new chapter in its timeless saga.

Discipline of Organising and Cataloging Prop Collections

The thrill of acquiring new props is often accompanied by the responsibility of preserving, showcasing, and managing them meticulously. Organising and cataloging is not just about creating an orderly display; it's about embracing the narratives behind each piece and ensuring that they resonate through time. So, as we embark on this journey of collection mastery, let's delve into the intricate art of keeping things impeccably cataloged and organised.

1. **The Digital Renaissance in Collection:**

   Move over, bulky binders and hand-scribbled notes! The modern collector leans on digital inventory management systems. These platforms are a haven for cataloging, with features that include image archiving, detailed tagging, and intuitive search options. Imagine the luxury of locating that coveted prop from a 1970's cult classic with just a couple of keystrokes!

   Advanced Features to Consider:

   - **Value Tracking:** Monitor the appreciation (or depreciation) of your items.
   - **Maintenance Alerts:** Never miss a cleaning or restoration session.

- **Virtual Exhibits:** Curate digital showcases, perfect for sharing with other enthusiasts or for insurance purposes.

2. **Crafting Prop Narratives:**

Every prop carries a legacy, a tale of its cinematic journey. This story enhances its value, both monetary and sentimental. Detailed documentation that includes its provenance, the scenes it graced, any accolades, and intriguing trivia creates a rich tapestry that fellow collectors and viewers will appreciate.

Level Up with Multimedia:

Capture your props in high resolution, or better yet, film them in recreated iconic scenes or themed dioramas. This visual element not only amplifies the prop's appeal but also serves as a testament to its authenticity.

3. **Safeguarding the Testimony of Time:** Props, while often robust on the big screen, can be delicate and prone to the ravages of time. Chart out a preservation strategy for your collection:

- **Handling Guidelines:** Use gloves for sensitive items. Handle with care.

- **Environmental Controls:** Maintain stable temperature and humidity. Protect from direct sunlight.

- **Archival Storage:** Invest in acid-free materials, especially for delicate props like scripts or clothing.

- **Routine Checks:** Regularly dust and inspect for any signs of degradation or pests.

In Closing:

While the task of cataloging and organising might seem daunting, it's an enriching experience that deepens your bond with your collection. It's not just about neat rows and labeled shelves; it's a passionate pursuit of preserving cinematic history in your very own sanctuary. So, armed with these tips, digital tools, and a zest for storytelling, go forth and curate a collection that not only wows but also narrates tales of its grandeur!

17

Preservation and Maintenance

Preservation and Maintenance

Preserving the life of your cherished props is paramount for every collector. These items, bearing tales from distant lands or nostalgic memories, deserve nothing but the utmost care. Let's dive into the world of preservation and maintenance to ensure these relics continue to tell their stories for generations to come.

The Delicate Art of Prop Handling
Understanding how to handle props is fundamental to their longevity. Every touch, every movement can either add to or take away from their lifespan.

- Gloves – Your Prop's Best Friend:

Imagine wielding a prop from a cherished movie scene. Before getting lost in the moment, ensure your gloves are on. They act as a barrier, protecting props from the oils and moisture on our hands.

- The Fragility Factor:

Props, much like heirlooms, need a delicate touch. For those made of materials like glass, ceramics, or intricate fabrics, ensure minimal direct contact. Using support structures, like display stands or foam paddings, will help reduce any risk of unintended damage.

- **The Golden Rule – No Edibles:**

Eating or drinking while admiring props might seem tempting, but the potential for accidents is too high a risk. Keep food and beverages away to prevent any unfortunate incidents.

- **Beware of the Elements:**

Environmental factors can be detrimental. Protect your props from sunlight, moisture, and dust. Using UV-protective casings, positioning away from windows, and cleaning with non-abrasive materials can shield them effectively.

- **Expert Advice is Golden:**

If ever in doubt about your prop's authenticity or its handling, turn to an expert. Join forums, connect with seasoned collectors, and never be afraid to seek advice.

Cleaning and Maintenance Masterclass

Essential Products:

Choosing the right cleaning agents is vital to ensure your props remain untarnished.

1. **Gentle Cleaning Solutions:**

   Use mild detergents or soap for delicate materials, testing them on a hidden spot first.

2. **Microfibre Cloths:**

   These lint-free cloths are perfect for wiping props without causing scratches.

3. **Isopropyl Alcohol:**

   Ideal for cleaning props of plastic, glass, or metal, it helps remove stubborn marks.

4. **Compressed Air:**

A great solution for intricate props, it clears dust and debris without physical contact.

Techniques to Master:

1. **Dusting:**

   A soft brush or microfibre cloth is excellent for dust removal.
2. **Stain Removal:**

   Different stains require different tactics. Always spot-test any cleaning solution.
3. **Steam Cleaning:**

A great option for moisture-resistant props, it loosens grime, making cleaning easier.

Protection against Deterioration:

1. **Storage Solutions:**

   Display props away from sunlight and extreme conditions. Consider using archival boxes for added safety.
2. **Proper Handling:**

   Always ensure clean, dry hands and, if needed, wear cotton gloves.
3. **Balanced Cleaning:**

   Regular cleaning is necessary, but overdoing can be harmful.
4. **Safe Environments:** Keep props in places free from excessive dust or pollutants. Using air purifiers can be beneficial.

Props are more than just collectables. They are memories, stories, and cherished belongings. Proper care and maintenance ensure they remain vibrant, holding their tales intact.

Disclaimer:

The guidelines and recommendations provided herein are for informational purposes only. If you have any doubts or concerns about cleaning or handling your prop, especially if it's rare, valuable, or of significant sentimental value, always consult with a professional conservator or expert in the field of prop preservation. Direct application of any cleaning method without professional advice could lead to unintended damage or deterioration of your item. Always prioritise the integrity and safety of your prop over any cleaning or maintenance attempt.

18

The Intricate Craft of Prop Restoration and Conservation

The Intricate Craft of Prop Restoration and Conservation

When delving into the world of prop collecting, enthusiasts quickly realise that the journey doesn't just stop at acquiring these cherished artefacts. Ensuring their longevity and preservation becomes equally paramount. This commitment often introduces collectors to the intricate realms of prop restoration and conservation.

When to Seek Expert Intervention

While a genuine love for the craft may motivate collectors to undertake restoration themselves, discernment is crucial. If a prop has significant historical value, monetary worth, or is damaged beyond basic repair, expert intervention becomes necessary.

Consider this scenario: you've procured a unique lightsaber prop from a renowned sci-fi saga. However, it showcases evident wear and tear. Rather than risking further damage with DIY methods, trusting a restoration expert ensures that every detail, from a crack to a faded hue, is meticulously attended to without compromising the prop's integrity.

Locating Professionals in the Prop Restoration Realm

Thankfully, the prop collecting world is a vibrant community teeming with dedicated experts and aficionados. To locate a restoration professional, consider the following:

- **Engage with the community:** Join forums, attend conventions, or reach out to veteran collectors. Their personal experiences and recommendations can lead you to trustworthy experts.

- **Do your research:** Once you've shortlisted potential professionals, delve into their portfolios. Gauge their expertise by evaluating their past restoration projects.

Deciphering Restoration vs. Conservation

It's vital to differentiate between restoration and conservation. While the former pertains to repairing and rejuvenating, the latter emphasises prevention and preservation.

Restoration is an intricate dance of mending while retaining authenticity. A prop restorer will, for instance, ensure that any added materials are reversible or seamlessly integrate with the original piece without compromising its essence.

Conservation, meanwhile, is a proactive approach. It revolves around creating an environment conducive to a prop's longevity, such as shielding a vintage movie poster from harmful UV rays or ensuring optimal humidity levels for fabric-based props.

The art of prop restoration and conservation is a labor of love, demanding a meticulous blend of skill, knowledge, and passion. By collaborating with seasoned professionals, you not only ensure that these storied items regain their splendour but also lay the foundation for their tales to be celebrated by future aficionados.

One of the best restorers in the business is: tomspinadesigns.com, Tom Spina Designs, Inc. specializes in creating custom statues, sculpture, mannequins, unique themed furniture and decor, and the restoration and display of film props and costumes.

19

Demystifying Prop Authentication: The Importance of Authenticity and Certificates of Authenticity (COA's)

Demystifying Prop Authentication: The Importance of Authenticity and Certificates of Authenticity (COA's)

The distinction between an authentic artefact and a skilled reproduction is paramount. This is where prop authentication comes to the forefront, acting as a beacon of trustworthiness and genuineness. Here's a deeper dive into the intricate process and why it holds significance.

What is Prop Authentication?

Simply put, prop authentication is the meticulous process that determines whether a prop truly originates from its purported source, be it a renowned movie, a popular TV show, an iconic stage production, or any other entertainment medium.

The Cornerstones of Prop Authentication:

1. **Expert Evaluation:** The world of props is vast and varied, and mastering its nuances requires dedication. Seasoned experts, with years of experience under their belt, are adept at discerning the minutiae that distinguish genuine props from reproductions. Their expansive access to resources, including databases, archives, and other reference materials, further amplifies their capability. As a tip for collectors, always seek recommendations or reviews before consulting an expert to ensure their credibility.

2. **Visual Inspection:** This is often the first line of defence in authentication. Experts meticulously scrutinise a prop for telltale signs of its origins. For instance, matching a prop with stills from a movie or comparing its craftsmanship with production notes can provide substantial evidence of its authenticity. An essential hint for collectors is to maintain a repository of references, like photographs or video footage, which can be instrumental during the authentication process.

3. **Scientific Analysis:** Sometimes, the naked eye isn't enough. Modern technology steps in to provide empirical evidence of a prop's lineage. Techniques like carbon dating, predominantly used for organic materials like wood or fabric, provide an age bracket for the prop, adding another layer to its authentication. Meanwhile, material analysis delves into the prop's very fabric. For a prop purportedly from the 1950s, the absence of materials or compounds not available during that era would raise red flags.

Certificates of Authenticity (COA's):

A COA serves as a tangible testament to a prop's authenticity. Typically issued by recognised experts or institutions, it affirms that the prop has undergone rigorous examination and has met specific criteria to be deemed genuine. As a tip for avid collectors, always store COAs in a safe place, and when considering a purchase, request to see the COA to ensure the prop's provenance.

Navigating the Nuances:

It's paramount to remember that prop authentication, while grounded in expertise and technology, isn't infallible. The realm is riddled with exceptional reproductions and contentious items. This inherent uncertainty underscores the importance of diligence, research, and trusting renowned experts. Engaging in informed discussions, attending collector's forums, and constantly updating one's knowledge can also empower collectors in their pursuit of genuine artefacts.

As the adage goes, knowledge is power.

20

Navigating the World of Prop Collecting: Identifying Reproductions and Ensuring Authenticity

Navigating the World of Prop Collecting: Identifying Reproductions and Ensuring Authenticity

The allure of holding a piece of cinematic history is undeniable. Who wouldn't want to have a lightsaber from Star Wars or the magical wand from Harry Potter in their collection? As passionate prop collectors, the excitement of such finds is palpable. However, lurking behind genuine artefacts are the shadows of deceitful reproductions. As you embark on this fascinating journey, it's essential to hone your skills in discerning genuine pieces from clever fakes.

Mastering the Art of Detection

1. **Understanding Red Flags:** Certain signs instantly hint at a prop's dubious origins. One primary red flag is subpar craftsmanship. Authentic props, designed for movies and shows, boast impeccable detail. On the contrary, reproductions may exhibit uneven paint, inferior materials, or imprecise dimensions. Tip: Use a magnifying glass or a jewellers loupe to scrutinise intricate details.

2. **Spotting Inconsistencies:** Fakes often have minor oversights that can betray them. Be it a misplaced logo, incorrect font, or an erroneous design element, these inconsistencies can help you identify a counterfeit. Advice: Maintain a database or repository of reference images and details for props you're interested in. This repository can be invaluable in cross-referencing.

3. **Decoding Artificial Ageing:** A favourite tactic of counterfeiters is to distress props, giving them an illusion of age and thus, authenticity. Genuine wear and tear have a natural pattern, while artificial ageing can seem forced or out of place. Hint: Check for patterns of wear that align with how the prop would have been used or handled.

4. **The 'Switcheroo' Tactic:** Counterfeiters might modify genuine props by replacing essential parts, cleverly masking their deceit. To counter this, be familiar with every aspect of the original prop. Remember, comprehensive research is your best defence against this trick.

Equip Yourself with Knowledge

Attending workshops or seminars on prop collecting can amplify your understanding. Engage with reputable dealers, join collectors' forums, and immerse yourself in discussions to gain insights from seasoned collectors.

Trust, but Verify

While it's essential to build relationships with sellers and dealers, always ensure that props come with provenance or a Certificate of Authenticity (COA). Even then, it's wise to do your due diligence, as COAs themselves can be forged.

The realm of prop collecting is undeniably enchanting, bridging us with moments of cinematic brilliance. While the thrill of hunting genuine artefacts is unmatched, it's crucial to stay vigilant. After all, the real magic lies in holding a piece of genuine history, untouched by the blemishes of deceit.

21

Case Studies: Famous Authentication Disputes

Case Studies: Famous Authentication Disputes

Authentication is crucial since genuine movie props can fetch significant sums of money. Here are some famous movie prop authentication disputes:

1. **The Ruby Slippers from "The Wizard of Oz":**
   - **Background:** Several pairs of ruby slippers were made for the 1939 film, but only a few are known to exist today. The whereabouts of some pairs are known, but others have mysteriously vanished, leading to claims and counterclaims over their authenticity.
   - **Dispute:** In 2005, a pair of slippers was found in a memorabilia store, leading to questions about their authenticity. After investigation, it was determined that these were one of the genuine pairs used during screen tests.
   - **Outcome:** The shoes were authenticated, and they've since

been displayed at various exhibitions. Another pair, stolen from the Judy Garland Museum in 2005, was recovered in 2018.

2. **Han Solo's Blaster from "Star Wars":**

   - **Background:** Props from the Star Wars saga are among the most sought-after items in the collector's world.

   - **Dispute:** In 2013, a blaster purported to be the one used by Harrison Ford's character, Han Solo, in "The Empire Strikes Back" and "Return of the Jedi," was put up for auction. The authenticity of the blaster became a topic of discussion among fans and collectors.

   - **Outcome:** After detailed examination and the presentation of provenance, the blaster was deemed authentic and fetched over $200,000 at auction.

3. **Orson Welles' "Citizen Kane" Oscar:**

   - **Background:** Although not a prop, Orson Welles' Oscar for "Citizen Kane" has an interesting history. After being believed lost or stolen for years, it resurfaced in the 1980s.

   - **Dispute:** When the Oscar reappeared, the Academy of Motion Picture Arts and Sciences claimed ownership, arguing that Welles had signed an agreement that if he sold it, he would offer it to the Academy for $1. However, there was no clear record of this agreement.

   - **Outcome:** After years of legal battles, the Oscar was returned to the Welles estate, and in 2011, it was auctioned for over $860,000.

4. **The Maltese Falcon Statue:**

   - **Background:** This statue from the classic 1941 film of the same name is one of the most iconic props in cinema history.

   - **Dispute:** Over the years, several falcon statues have been claimed to be the original. The dispute over authenticity arose due to the existence of multiple falcons - some made of lead, others of resin - for different scenes in the movie.

- **Outcome:** The bona fide lead statue, weighing 45 pounds, was authenticated and sold at a Bonhams auction in New York in 2013 for over $4 million.

These disputes underscore the importance of thorough authentication and provenance in the prop collecting world. As values soar, so does the temptation for counterfeits and the ensuing disputes over authenticity.

22

Most Iconic & Expensive Movie Props

Movie props, especially from iconic films, have always captivated audiences and collectors alike. Over the years, various props have been auctioned or sold for impressive sums. Here are ten of the most iconic and expensive movie props in history:

1. **Ruby Slippers from "The Wizard of Oz" (1939)**

   * The ruby slippers worn by Judy Garland in this classic film are among the most recognised movie props ever. Multiple pairs were made for the film, and one of the few known remaining pairs was auctioned in 2012 for over $2 million. These shoes symbolise Dorothy's journey and the magic of the silver screen.

2. **Aston Martin DB5 from "Goldfinger" (1964)**

   * James Bond's cars are legendary, but the Aston Martin DB5 stands out. Used in multiple Bond films, this car, complete with gadgets, was sold at auction in 2010 for $4.6 million.

3. **Marilyn Monroe's Dress from "The Seven Year Itch" (1955)**

   * The ivory pleated dress worn by Marilyn Monroe during the iconic subway grate scene sold at auction in 2011 for $5.6

million. The scene and the dress have become emblematic of Hollywood allure.

4. **Harrison Ford's Blaster from "Blade Runner" (1982)**

   * This iconic prop, wielded by Harrison Ford's character Rick Deckard, is a symbol of the neo-noir sci-fi genre. It was sold in 2019 for over $200,000.

5. **The Maltese Falcon Statue from "The Maltese Falcon" (1941)**

   * The heavy prop, pivotal to the plot of this classic noir film starring Humphrey Bogart, fetched over $4 million at auction in 2013.

6. **Han Solo's Blaster from "Star Wars: Return of the Jedi" (1983)**

   * Star Wars memorabilia frequently fetches high prices, but Han Solo's blaster stands out. It sold at auction in 2018 for $550,000.

7. **The Cowardly Lion's Costume from "The Wizard of Oz" (1939)**

   * Another iconic prop from the world of Oz, the Cowardly Lion's costume, made of real lion pelts, sold in 2014 for over $3 million.

8. **Audrey Hepburn's Dress from "Breakfast at Tiffany's" (1961)**

   * The elegant black Givenchy dress worn by Audrey Hepburn as Holly Golightly is one of the most recognisable in film history. In 2006, it was sold for approximately $900,000, with proceeds going to charity.

9. **Von Trapp Drapery Outfits from "The Sound of Music" (1965)**

   * The outfits made from drapes that Maria and the children wear during the "Do-Re-Mi" sequence were sold at auction in 2013 for $1.56 million.

10. **Wilson the Volleyball from "Cast Away" (2000)**

* The face-painted volleyball became an iconic symbol of Tom Hanks' isolation in the film. In 2001, Wilson was auctioned off for $18,500.

And one last noteworthy mention:

DeLorean from "Back to the Future" (1985)

- The DeLorean DMC-12, often simply referred to as "the DeLorean," is perhaps one of the most iconic vehicles in cinematic history. The car's gull-wing doors, stainless steel exterior, and transformation into a time machine by the eccentric Dr. Emmett Brown have solidified its place in pop culture. In the "Back to the Future" trilogy, the DeLorean serves not merely as a mode of transport but as a central character, facilitating Marty McFly's time-traveling adventures.

- The original DeLorean used in the film has been displayed at the Petersen Automotive Museum in Los Angeles. There were multiple DeLorean models used during the filming of the trilogy, with each serving different purposes: some for stunts, some for interior shots, and others for the various modifications that the car undergoes throughout the series.

- In terms of value, in 2011, the DeLorean used in the third instalment of the trilogy, which was owned by co-writer and producer Bob Gale, was restored and auctioned off. It fetched a staggering $541,000. The proceeds from the sale went to the Michael J. Fox Foundation for Parkinson's Research. Given the car's continued popularity and cultural significance, it's safe to say that its value has likely appreciated over the years.

- The DeLorean's pop culture status also means that it's a popular item among replica builders. Authentic details, like the flux capacitor, time circuit controls, and even Mr. Fusion Home Energy Reactor, are often added to capture the true essence of the cinematic machine. However, collectors and fans should be cautious about the authenticity of any "original" movie DeLoreans up for sale. As with any valuable movie prop, there are replicas and counterfeits in the market.

The DeLorean from "Back to the Future" remains a symbol of 1980s cinema and the fascinating concept of time travel. Its blend of science fiction with the quintessential American adventure story ensures that it will remain a sought-after collectible for generations to come.

Star Wars lightsabers—often referred to as "light sabers" or "light savers" colloquially—are among the most iconic and sought-after movie props. These items can be quite valuable depending on several factors, such as who used the lightsaber in the movie, its condition, its provenance (i.e., its history of ownership and documentation proving its authenticity), and its importance to the plot of the movie.

Original lightsabers from the earlier Star Wars films (Episode IV: A New Hope, Episode V: The Empire Strikes Back, and Episode VI: Return of the Jedi) often command the highest prices. Here are a few notable sales:

1. Luke Skywalker's Lightsaber: In 2017, a lightsaber described as being used by Mark Hamill's character, Luke Skywalker, in the first two Star Wars films sold for $450,000.

2. Obi-Wan Kenobi's Lightsaber: Sir Alec Guinness's lightsaber from the original Star Wars film was auctioned for a considerable sum as well, with reports varying but often falling in the $200,000–$300,000 range.

3. Darth Vader's Lightsaber: The dark side is also popular among collectors. Darth Vader's lightsaber has sold for over $100,000 in past auctions.

4. Anakin Skywalker's Lightsaber: Anakin's lightsaber from Episode III: Revenge of the Sith sold for around $135,000.

Note that these numbers can vary, and there are also many replicas and non-authentic versions out there. Collectors are generally most interested in props that were actually used during filming, as verified by solid documentation and certificates of authenticity.

Always do your research and consult with experts when possible. The world of prop collecting is fascinating but can be fraught with forgeries and exaggerated claims.

These props hold more than just monetary value; they are pieces of cinematic history, embodying the essence of films that have left an indelible mark on global popular culture.

23

Stolen Props

Stolen Props:

Whilst writing this book I came across an article on the theft of props from the Beetlejuice 2 set, I have written about it below.

A significant theft has occurred on the set of "Beetlejuice 2," leading to the disappearance of an iconic statue originally featured in Tim Burton's 1988 cult classic film. According to an official report from the Vermont State Police, the statue was stolen in conjunction with a lamppost adorned with a unique pumpkin ornament.

In a recent social media update, Vermont State Police humorously noted, "Reciting the statue's name three times did not result in its reappearance." Authorities are actively investigating the theft of the 150-pound set piece from the film's shooting location in East Corinth, Vermont. The lamppost, distinguished by its pumpkin decoration, was also taken.

The theft reportedly took place between 5 p.m. on Thursday, July 13, and 11 a.m. on Monday, July 17, during on-location filming in

Vermont. Per a report by NBC 5, the suspects drove an older-model GMC pickup truck to the set. They initially removed the base of the lamppost shortly after midnight on July 14 and subsequently loaded it onto their vehicle. Security personnel have reported that the thieves returned to the set on Monday to abscond with the statue.

The theft of movie props is not uncommon, and some famous examples have made headlines over the years. While some of these stolen items have been recovered, others remain missing:

1. Ruby Slippers from "The Wizard of Oz" - These iconic slippers were recovered in 2018 after being stolen from the Judy Garland Museum in 2005.

2. Iron Man Suit - Disappeared from a Los Angeles storage facility in 2018, the suit was valued at $325,000.

3. Aston Martin DB5 from "Goldfinger" - Stolen from a Florida airport hangar in 1997, this James Bond car remains missing.

4. Props from "Star Wars" - Items including a stormtrooper helmet were stolen but later recovered.

5. Indiana Jones' Whip - Reported stolen but eventually returned.

6. Orca Tooth from "Jaws" - Taken from a Planet Hollywood restaurant, this prop was later returned.

7. Props from "Harry Potter" Films - Various items, such as wands and the golden snitch, have been stolen.

8. Marilyn Monroe Dress from "The Seven Year Itch" - Stolen from a Beverly Hills home in 1993 and still missing.

9. Treasure Map from "The Goonies" - Mistakenly discarded by Sean Astin's mother, Patty Duke.

10. Sex Toys from "Pain & Gain" - Purchased for a warehouse scene, these items began disappearing before they could be returned.

11. Maschinenmensch from "Metropolis" - The robot in Fritz Lang's 1927 film has influenced everyone from Kraftwerk to Janelle Monáe but the original prop didn't survive the shoot. Some claim it was destroyed during production but its actual fate remains unknown.

12. Motorcycles from "Easy Rider" - Three out of four custom-built choppers were stolen prior to the film's release; the remaining bike was auctioned but its authenticity was later questioned.

13. Golden Gun from "The Man with the Golden Gun" - One of the prop guns, valued at $136,000, was stolen from Elstree Studios in 2008.

14. Chevy Chevelle Malibu from "Pulp Fiction" - Stolen in 1994, this car was discovered 19 years later in an unrelated police investigation.

15. Spider-Man Suits from "Spider-Man" - Four suits, each valued at $50,000, were stolen in 2001. At least three were later recovered, and arrests were made.

16. Fibreglass Cows from "World War Z" - These props went missing from a filming location in 2011; however, local police were not officially notified.

Due to their cultural, historical, and monetary significance, these stolen or missing movie props have often led to intricate investigations and captivated public interest. They are highly sought after in both the black market and among private collectors.

24

Actors Who Retained Props from Their Film Projects

Notable Actors Who Appropriated Memorabilia from Their Film Sets

Several actors have openly disclosed taking home props from their respective film projects over the years. The items range from uniquely crafted custom-made props to more modest memorabilia. Below are some notable examples:

Eddie Redmayne: Newt's Briefcase from 'Fantastic Beasts'
Eddie Redmayne, who portrays Newt Scamander in the "Fantastic Beasts" series, admitted to pilfering Newt's signature briefcase from the set. Despite the ambiguous future of the franchise, Redmayne was able to secure this keepsake before production came to a pause.

Mark Hamill: Various 'Star Wars' Props

Mark Hamill, the actor behind Luke Skywalker, has amassed quite a collection of "Star Wars" memorabilia over the years. His collection includes a Stormtrooper helmet, elements of C-3PO, and other iconic props. Hamill often showcases these items on social media.

Sam Neill: Alan Grant's Boots from 'Jurassic Park'

Sam Neill, known for his role as Dr. Alan Grant in "Jurassic Park," intentionally walked off the set wearing his character's boots. His co-star, Laura Dern, also confessed to keeping an amber ring from the original film.

Adam Driver: Kylo Ren's Lightsaber

Adam Driver, who played Kylo Ren in the "Star Wars" sequels, has also taken props from various films. Among these is a lightsaber from one of the "Star Wars" sequels, along with other artefacts from "The Last Duel."

Margot Robbie: Harley Quinn's Baseball Bat

Margot Robbie, who plays Harley Quinn in the DC Extended Universe, took home the anti-hero's signature baseball bat. Robbie disclosed that she keeps it next to her bed as a cautionary measure against intruders.

Tom Holland: E.D.I.T.H Glasses from 'Spider-Man: Far From Home'

Tom Holland, the current face of Spider-Man, took home Tony Stark's E.D.I.T.H glasses. Despite the prop's importance in the narrative, Holland managed to walk away with this piece of memorabilia.

Andrew Garfield: Spider-Man Suit from 'The Amazing Spider-Man 2'

Contrary to Holland, Andrew Garfield successfully acquired a Spider-Man suit from the set of "The Amazing Spider-Man 2," a feat that Holland was unable to accomplish.

Will Ferrell: Prosthetic Testicles from 'Step Brothers'
Will Ferrell kept the prosthetic testicles used in a memorable scene from "Step Brothers." Ferrell has admitted to utilising them for comedic purposes at dinner parties.

Aaron Paul: Various Props from 'Breaking Bad' and 'El Camino'
Aaron Paul, who portrayed Jesse Pinkman in "Breaking Bad," took various props, including a letter to the character Brock from the film "El Camino."

Chris Hemsworth: Thor's Hammer, Mjolnir
Chris Hemsworth took home Thor's hammer, Mjolnir, but later lost it. This came to light when his co-star, Jeremy Renner, publicly disclosed the actors who took props from the "Avengers" set.

These actors, either by sentiment or for other reasons, have amassed collections that serve as tangible reminders of their roles, often becoming valuable film memorabilia.

25

Most Memorable & Collectible TV Show Props

TV shows, especially those with a long run or significant cultural impact, have produced some highly memorable props that have become iconic in the world of collectibles. Here are some of the most memorable and collectible TV show props:

1. **The TARDIS (Doctor Who)**

   - The blue police box is instantly recognisable around the world, even to those who aren't fans of the show. It's been a central figure of "Doctor Who" since its inception in 1963.

2. **KITT (Knight Rider)**

   - The talking Pontiac Trans Am known as KITT (Knight Industries Two Thousand) is one of the most iconic TV vehicles of all time, making it a prized collectible.

3. **The Iron Throne (Game of Thrones)**

   - This imposing throne, made of swords, was the seat of

power in the Seven Kingdoms, and replica versions have become quite popular among fans.

4. **The Robot (Lost in Space)**

   - Known for the line "Danger, Will Robinson!", the Robot has become synonymous with classic sci-fi TV.

5. **Captain Kirk's Command Chair (Star Trek: The Original Series)**

   - The central seat on the bridge of the USS Enterprise, from where Captain James T. Kirk gave his orders, is iconic in the realm of sci-fi props.

6. **Buffy's Stake (Buffy the Vampire Slayer)**

   - Buffy's wooden stake, called "Mr. Pointy," is emblematic of the show's mix of action, drama, and humour.

7. **Lucille (The Walking Dead)**

   - The barbed-wire-wrapped baseball bat that became the signature weapon of the antagonist Negan is both feared and revered by fans of the series.

8. **The Central Perk Couch (Friends)**

   - This orange couch from the fictional coffee shop "Central Perk" became a staple setting for the cast of "Friends" and is instantly recognisable to fans of the show.

9. **Dexter's Blood Slide Box (Dexter)**

   - Forensic expert and serial killer Dexter Morgan kept mementos of his victims in the form of blood slides. The box containing these slides is iconic for fans of the show.

10. **The Fonz's Leather Jacket (Happy Days)**

- Henry Winkler's character, Arthur "Fonzie" Fonzarelli, popularised the leather jacket, making it an emblem of cool for an entire generation.

Many of these props, especially original versions or limited-edition replicas, can fetch significant prices in the collectibles market. Their iconic nature ensures that they remain in demand among fans and collectors.

26

Collectors Stories

Collectors Stories

Cortez Castillo

Cortez traces the genesis of his passion for film prop collecting back to his childhood, captivated by the film "Arachnophobia."

The first prop he ever acquired was a static "Baby Bob" spider from this very movie. 'I was so enamoured with the film as a kid that I believe it kickstarted my lifelong fascination with film props,' Cortez shares. He didn't stop at just one; that initial purchase eventually multiplied into four of the same spiders.

Although his collection has since expanded to include a diverse array of pieces from various films, Cortez fondly acknowledges that these little spiders were the catalysts for his ever-growing collection.

Eric Anthony Leong

Eric, a cornerstone in the community of film prop enthusiasts.

Eric serves as one of the moderators at 'Inexpensive Screen Used Movie Props $100 Or Less,' sharing his insights and expertise with collectors both seasoned and new.

A multifaceted individual, Eric is not just a moderator but also a Dad, Artist, and Entrepreneur who has made significant contributions to the world of entertainment.

His professional portfolio is impressive, having served as a Prop Fabricator on 'Fear the Walking Dead,' an Armorer and Fabricator in the Film and Television Industry, a former Propmaster for 'Where All Light Tends To Go,' and an Assistant Propmaster for 'Young Dylan.'

To explore more about his work and journey, visit his website at ericanthonyproductions.com.

Jimmy Olsen from the MOVIE PROPS - REPLICAS - STUDIO SCALE MODELS - FIGURES forum.

I have been an avid collector of Teenage Mutant Ninja Turtles (TMNT) memorabilia since the age of 13, specialising particularly in the Playmates toy line released between 1989 and 1998. Over the years, I have had the privilege of interacting with several key individuals associated with the TMNT franchise, such as Kevin Eastman, Peter Laird, and Steve Lavigne. This has enriched my understanding of various aspects of TMNT, including the intricacies of movie props related to the series.

In pursuit of my passion for collecting, I have divested portions of my toy collection to focus on acquiring and restoring movie props from the TMNT franchise. Notably, I possess a fully restored stunt suit of Venus de Milo, the female Ninja Turtle, which was featured in the Teenage Mutant Ninja Turtles: The Next Mutation FX series. My collection also includes a plethora of other significant TMNT props, meticulously documented and archived on multiple backup tablets and computers.

While the journey has been overwhelmingly fulfilling, collecting has its inherent risks. For instance, I made an investment in bo staffs, which were purportedly used in the second TMNT film by stunt actor David Leif Tilden. Unfortunately, I later discovered these items were likely not authentic, resulting in an unsellable inventory.

Nevertheless, my journey in collecting, restoring, and owning TMNT memorabilia has been incredibly rewarding. I have met a diverse array of individuals, acquired remarkable items, and even learned valuable lessons from less successful ventures.

NOTE: I did try to include the photos kindly provided by the above contributors but Ingramsparks uploading service would not allow me to move forward with approving the print file if the photos were included. So please go the forums above to see the excellent props for sale, made and uploaded by these talented individuals.

27

Notable Websites Worldwide

Prop collecting is a specialised field, and the websites dedicated to it can vary based on the type of props, their authenticity, and price range. Here's a list of notable websites worldwide where prop collectors might find items to purchase:

1. **Prop Store** (https://www.propstore.com/)

   - One of the leading film and TV memorabilia companies worldwide, with offices in London and Los Angeles. They offer a vast range of original items from various movies and shows.
2. **The Golden Closet** (http://www.thegoldencloset.com/)

   - A premier retailer for screen used wardrobe, props, and music entertainment memorabilia.
3. **Movie Prop Warehouse** (https://moviepropwarehouse.com)

   - Based in the UK, this website offers a wide variety of genuine film props and costumes.
4. **Profiles in History** (https://profilesinhistory.com/)

   - Located in California, they've established themselves as the world's largest auctioneer of original Hollywood memorabilia.

5. **ScreenUsed** (http://www.screenused.com/)

    - They offer both auctions and fixed-price items, with a large selection from various movies.

6. **eBay** (https://www.ebay.com)

    - While eBay is a general auction site, there is a significant market for movie props here. However, due diligence is crucial because not every listing will be authentic.

7. **Premiere Props** (http://www.premiereprops.com/)

    - A major Hollywood prop retailer that also holds live auctions.

8. **YourProps** (http://www.yourprops.com/)

    - While primarily a platform for prop collectors to showcase their collection, some listings are for sale or trade.

9. **Propabilia** (https://www.propabilia.com/)

    - A movie prop auction website that has been around for many years.

10. **Reel Clothes & Props** (http://www.reelclothes.com/)

    - Specialises in original wardrobe and props from movies and TV shows.

Remember, when buying from any website, it's crucial to do your own due diligence. Check the site's authenticity guarantees, ask for provenance or Certificates of Authenticity (COA), and always be wary of deals that seem too good to be true.

Websites to obtain COA help & authentication :

When it comes to prop authentication, the value of a reputable source cannot be overstated. Here's a list of websites and companies that offer authentication services and Certificate of Authenticity (COA) for movie and TV show props:

1. **Prop Store** ([propstore.com](https://www.propstore.com/))

    - One of the industry's leading film and TV memorabilia companies, they offer a wide range of items with a COA.

2. **Profiles in History** ([profilesinhistory.com](https://profilesin-history.com/))

   - A well-known dealer in collectible Hollywood memorabilia. They offer authentication services and their items come with a COA.
3. **The Prop Block** ([thepropblock.com](https://www.theprop-block.com/))

   - Provides certified screen used film & television props from various studios.
4. **Movie Prop Warehouse** ([moviepropware-house.com](http://moviepropwarehouse.com/))

   - Known for their original movie props and costumes, they offer COAs with every item.
5. **Heroes & Legends** ([heroesandlegends.net](http://www.he-roesandlegends.net/))

   - While they focus on autographs, they do handle movie memorabilia and offer COA services.
6. **PSA/DNA Authentication Services** ([psac-ard.com](https://www.psacard.com/))

   - Primarily for autograph authentication, they're one of the most recognised names in the industry. They occasionally handle movie memorabilia and props.
7. **James Spence Authentication (JSA)** ([spence-loa.com](https://www.spenceloa.com/))

   - Like PSA/DNA, JSA focuses mainly on autograph authentication but does occasionally handle movie-related items.
8. **YourProps** ([yourprops.com](http://www.yourprops.com/))

   - It's primarily a community-driven site where collectors can showcase their items. While not an authenticator per se, being in this community can guide collectors toward experts and resources for authentication.

9. **ScreenUsed** (screenused.com)

    - A dealer in screen-used Hollywood memorabilia. They provide COAs with their items and have a reputation for authentic pieces.

10. **Propabilia** ([propabilia.com](https://www.propabilia.com/))

- They handle props and costumes and provide authentication and COAs for their items.

And the most popular and respected is:

Beckett Authentication Services (BAS) is the newest member of the Beckett Media portfolio. Since 1984, Beckett has been the industry standard for price guides, card grading, and now with the inception of BAS, autograph authentication.

World renowned autograph experts Steve Grad and Brian Sobrero bring their vast experience with autographs from all genres and eras to the forefront of BAS. They have authenticated some of the rarest and most valuable items in the industry, a testament to their level of expertise.

With a full range of services for your autograph collection, Beckett Authentication Services is the only authentication company you'll ever need.

Established November 2016.

When seeking authentication and a COA for a prop, always do due diligence on the company or individual offering the service. While the above-listed entities have solid reputations, there are many out there who may not be as scrupulous. If possible, seek recommendations from other collectors or industry professionals.

28

Acknowledgments

Acknowledgments

In the incredible journey of penning this book, there are certain stars that have shone the brightest, guiding and inspiring me each step of the way.

First and foremost, a monumental 'thank you' to the 'MOVIE PROPS - REPLICAS - STUDIO SCALE MODELS - FIGURES' forum on Facebook. This platform, teeming with passion and knowledge, has been invaluable. I am especially indebted to the moderator, Robert Cowley, for his ceaseless efforts and to all the forum members. You're captivating stories and the mesmerising photographs you shared have breathed life into this book.

Similarly, I wish to extend my deepest appreciation to the 'Inexpensive Screen Used Movie Props $100 Or Less' forum on Facebook. A heartfelt thank you to the dedicated moderator, Eric Anthony Leong, and all the forum members who generously contributed. Your insights and experiences have enriched this work beyond measure.

Special thanks must go to Jimmy Olson from the MOVIE PROPS - REPLICAS - STUDIO SCALE MODELS - FIGURES forum.

Jimmy's extensive collection of Teenage Mutant Ninja Turtles props and memorabilia, coupled with his generously contributed photographs and expertise, have been an invaluable resource in the creation of this book. His contributions have not only enriched the content but also added an unparalleled layer of authenticity and depth.

To Jimmy, your passion for collecting and your willingness to share your treasures have truly made a significant impact. Thank you for your incredible support.

Lastly, words might fall short, but I wish to convey the profound love and admiration I hold for all the prop masters and replica producers out there. The sheer artistry, the meticulous attention to detail, and the soul you pour into your creations is awe-inspiring.

Each piece you craft is not merely a prop or a replica; it is a testament to human ingenuity and skill, and nothing short of spectacular.

From the depths of my heart, thank you all for making this book a reality.

29

A Parting Note

A Parting Note

Dear Valued Reader,

As I pen down this final note, I'm overwhelmed with gratitude. The pages you've just journeyed through are more than mere words; they represent hours of passion, research, and a deep-seated love for the world of prop collecting.

The journey of prop collecting is as much about cherishing the past as it is about ensuring a legacy for the future. By curating, safeguarding, and narrating the stories of your props, you're not just a collector – you're a custodian of cinematic history. Celebrate every prop, narrate it's lore, and remember, every spotlight you cast adds a new chapter in its timeless saga.

Your decision to pick up this book, to invest your time and immerse yourself in its pages, has given my words purpose and life. I hope that somewhere between the lines, you found insights that resonated, stories that captivated, and perhaps a spark of inspiration for your own adventures in prop collecting.

I'd like to express my sincere thanks to every individual who has been part of this journey—be it my family, friends, fellow collectors, or those in the entertainment industry whose dedication brings stories to life on the screen. But most importantly, thank you, dear reader, for being the heartbeat of this endeavour.

As you close this book, know that our journey doesn't end here. The world of props is ever-evolving, filled with discoveries waiting just around the corner. I hope you venture forth with renewed enthusiasm, and perhaps one day, our paths will cross in a convention hall, an auction, or in the intricate web of shared stories and memories.

Until then, from the deepest recesses of my heart, thank you for reading, and happy collecting.

Warmly,

Asaf

30

Acknowledgment of Errors

Acknowledgment of Errors

In the pursuit of knowledge and the chronicling of stories, even with the best intentions and efforts, oversights may occur. It is with a profound sense of responsibility that I acknowledge any inaccuracies, errors, or omissions that may be present in this book. They are, in entirety, my own.

While every effort has been made to ensure the accuracy and completeness of the information contained within these pages, the dynamic nature of knowledge and human fallibility means imperfections are inevitable. I am deeply appreciative of the readers and experts in the field who engage with this work, and I welcome constructive feedback and corrections.

Your understanding and patience, as you embark on this journey with me, is both valued and cherished. I am committed to continuous learning, and any subsequent editions of this book will aim to rectify acknowledged errors. Thank you for your support and trust.